PAVILLON DE L'ESPRIT NOUVEAU: A 21st Century Show Home

Architecture and Design Series
Second Edition

SI

Contents

4   Introduction

13   Show Home
    Carson Chan

51   Going Green
    Shawn Maximo

54   Index
    Marc Matchak

103   Public Programs

105   Hot Property
    Trish Goff

110   Contributors

112   Acknowledgments

Introduction

In his manifesto *Towards a New Architecture*, Swiss architect Le
Corbusier entices readers with an enigmatic declaration: "The
outside is always an inside."[1] Although this statement regards
architectural planning, it also functions as a prescient summary
of twenty-first-century living: external presentation is a symp-
tom of a deliberate consciousness, and the distinction between
the public and private self has all but been obliterated. Echoing
Corbusier nearly seventy years later, architectural historian
Beatriz Colomina reaffirms "the exterior view depends on a view
of the interior."[2] It is through this understanding of the persis-
tent blurring of the inside and the outside that one experiences
PAVILLON DE L'ESPRIT NOUVEAU: A 21st Century Show Home (PDLEN).

When conceiving the exhibition, Felix Burrichter, its curator,
sought to probe how domesticity is articulated and experienced
today. As an homage to Corbusier's revolutionary ideas around
mass production and the mechanization of the home, Burrichter
thought of restaging Corbusier's 1925 exhibition *Pavillon de
l'Esprit Nouveau* as a show home filled with revolutionary
examples of forward-thinking contemporary design, most of
which could not have been made before the twenty-first century.
The space at Swiss Institute was organized into six loosely
delineated zones, each an irreverent update on a traditional
domestic layout. But, given Burrichter's multivalent vision,
his curatorial work did not end at the exhibition of objects.
In collaboration with the artist and exhibition designer Shawn
Maximo, he included a closed-circuit video-surveillance system
to capture viewers as they moved through each zone. Monitors
in each section displayed renderings of fantastical spaces
designed by Maximo into which the visitor was inserted. To
execute this surreal effect, the entire interior of Swiss
Institute was painted with industrial-grade chroma-key paint,
a vibrant green that enveloped the viewer. Each greenscreen
rendering was inspired by Corbusier's own droll sense of humor.
The dining room featured a giant spit-roasted marshmallow.
Marijuana and peyote plants populated the roof garden. The home
office doubled as an ultra-luxurious gym/server farm—a satirical
take on the storage and distribution of physical and computational
power. Implicit in what Burrichter describes as "digital escap-
ism" is the impulse to submit oneself to the public sphere.

The collapse of interior and exterior was evident in the cascade of selfies taken by visitors. In both premise and design, *PDLEN* provided a delightfully transgressive opportunity to be one's own Peeping Tom.

An exhibition so deeply rooted in the sensory experience predicated on one's body puts added pressure on the catalogue to uphold the spirit of engagement. Thanks to Burrichter's meticulous input, we feel this book does exactly that. It begins with an essay by architecture writer and curator Carson Chan on the abiding influence of the show home in the twenty-first century, followed by installation images and an essay by Maximo that recounts the highly detailed exhibition design. This essay is followed by an index, written by artist Marc Matchak, of every piece that populated the show home, providing a historical conceptualization of each. Considering the occasional absurdity that lurks beneath the exhibition's seductive images, it seems fitting that this book ends with a graphic version of the guided tour of *PDLEN* by its exclusive sales agent, Trish Goff. Follow Goff as she takes a selfie on RO/LU's four-poster mirrored bed, whips up a martini at Nanu Al-Hamad's *Med-Bar*, and sells her remaining four units in record time.

To this day, *PDLEN* remains one of the most highly attended exhibitions in Swiss Institute's thirty-two-year history, and it's easy to see why. Through their exhibition design and absolute commitment to innovation from both leading designers and emerging artists, Burrichter and Maximo fully embraced the mission of the SI Architecture and Design Series. As Colomina points out, "Architecture is not simply a platform that accommodates the viewing subject. It is a viewing mechanism that produces the subject. It precedes and frames its occupant."[3] With *PDLEN*, Burrichter transforms Colomina's theory into practice—that architecture does not simply contain, it sees. It develops and transports viewers—to an arid desert, to outer space, to the depths of the ocean. And while *PDLEN* presents an exacting summation of how we live now, it also alludes to architecture and design's ambiguous future. We hope this book serves as a guide as these speculative realities inch ever closer.

Simon Castets
Director, Swiss Institute

Notes

1. Le Corbusier, *Towards a New Architecture* (New York: Dover Publications, 1986), 180.

2. Beatriz Colomina, "Sexuality and Space," in *Sexuality and Space*, ed. Beatriz Colomina (New York: Princeton Architectural Press, 1992), 78.

3. Colomina, 83.

PAVILLON DE L'ESPRIT NOUVEAU: A 21st CENTURY SHOW HOME

CURATED BY FELIX BURRICHTER, EXHIBITION DESIGN BY SHAWN MAXIMO

LINDSEY ADELMAN	MARLIE MUL
NANU AL-HAMAD	IFEANYI OGANWU
ARANDA\LASCH	LEON RANSMEIER
ALESSANDRO BAVA	SEAN RASPET
JOSH BITELLI	JESSI REAVES
CAMILLE BLIN	GUTO REQUENA
LAURELINE GALLIOT	RO/LU
KONSTANTIN GRCIC	ROSSI BIANCHI
PAUL KOPKAU	JULIKA RUDELIUS
KRAM/WEISSHAAR	SOFT BAROQUE
JORIS LAARMAN	ROBERT STADLER
MAX LAMB	IAN STELL
LE CORBUSIER	KATIE STOUT
PIERO LISSONI	ELISA STROZYK
PHILIPPE MALOUIN	STUDIO DRIFT
SHAWN MAXIMO	PATRICIA URQUIOLA
JASPER MORRISON	CHRISTIAN WASSMANN
JONATHAN MUECKE	BETHAN LAURA WOOD

#PDLEN

THE 2015 ARCHITECTURE AND DESIGN EXHIBITION IS SUPPORTED BY THE GRAHAM FOUNDATI⬤
FOR ADVANCED STUDIES IN THE FINE ARTS, PRESENCE SWITZERLAND, AUSTRIAN CULTUR⬤
FORUM NEW YORK, KARA MANN AND CULTURAL PARTNER FONDATION LE CORBUSIER, PARI⬤
IN-KIND SUPPORT PROVIDED BY: AZNOM; CARPENTER'S WORKSHOP; DESIGNTEX; FLOS; GC⬤
LIVING DIVANI; MAHARAM; PANTONE; RESOLUME; ROSCO LABORATORIES; SOYLENT; US⬤
VITRA, USA.

Le Corbusier, *Pavillon de l'Esprit Nouveau, Paris, 1925*

Show Home

Carson Chan

PAVILLON DE L'ESPRIT NOUVEAU: A 21st Century Show Home was a home-furnishing show that borrowed its title from Le Corbusier's seminal pavilion at the 1925 Exposition des Arts Décoratifs et Industriels Modernes in Paris. The 2015 exhibition also acknowledged another milestone in the history of modern architecture, Sigfried Giedion's 700-page work *Mechanization Takes Command: A Contribution to Anonymous History,* assembling and thereby explaining what the architectural historian meant by the "anonymous history" of the time. Beyond the museums, villas, and grand urban plans that by the mid-twentieth century had become emblematic of modern architecture, Giedion was concerned with chairs, tables, beds, bathtubs, and kitchens—the objects and spaces that organized quotidian life and increasingly shaped the way humans engaged with the world.

Although the mechanization of the household in the mid-nineteenth century signaled the advent of a "servantless" gentry in Europe[1], critically, for Giedion, the mechanization of objects and systems that surround us indicated a broader, more essential shift in the manner in which humans live. As assembly lines replaced artisans and pastures made way for feedlots, the world we lived in and the world we imagined began to align. "Mechanization is the outcome of a mechanistic conception of the world," Giedion observed[2]. In this way, we inhabit and perpetuate a cycle. The Industrial Revolution and the subsequent increasing mechanization of daily lives was as much an entry into modes of efficiency, expediency, and excess as it was a cycling of mechanical logic into human processes. Neither good nor bad, for Giedion, "mechanization is an agent, like water, fire, light. It is blind and without direction of its own."[3] In scrutinizing the machines around us, we get to glimpse the disposition of the self-perpetuating systems of our own creation through which our "anonymous history" becomes individually authored and subjectively hewn.

The 2015 exhibition was conceived with as much affinity to *Die Wohnung unserer Zeit* (The Apartment of Our Times)—a 1931 showcase of full-scale house mock-ups in Berlin organized by Ludwig Mies van der Rohe—as with contemporary IKEA showrooms. It brings into play the unsettling thought that the things

Le Corbusier, *Pavillon de l'Esprit Nouveau*, Paris, 1925

sharing our intimacies and the objects that tell of our taste and self-image often enter our home as merchandise, retailed from an ever-expanding list of options. Networked infrastructures of commerce, communication, and security pervade contemporary living. With walls painted "video green," the exhibition design transformed Swiss Institute into a giant greenscreen and, in so doing, introduced metaphors of transmission, telepresence, and surveillance in the home. In each of the six spaces—living room, dining room, study, kitchen, bedroom, and outdoor patio—in lieu of framed artworks, there were flat-screen monitors show-ing nearby furnishings and visitors transported (chroma-keyed) into other places digitally, from desert scenes to panic rooms. If home shows have traditionally offered new ways to imagine our sense of home in the domestic realm, this exhibition seemed to say: "To be somewhere is to be somewhere else; to be inside is to be outside; to be at home is to be at work."

In this household scenario of twenty-four-hour self-observation and digital transportation, the most private places can also become the most public. In an essay titled "The Century of the Bed," the architecture scholar Beatriz Colomina argued that "the city has moved into the bed,"[4] citing a 2012 *Wall Street Journal* article which reported that 80 percent of young New York City professionals regularly worked from the place usually designated for sleeping. As distinctions between work and play erode and a machine logic of 24/7 capitalism (to paraphrase the historian Jonathan Crary) sets in, so do the boundaries of our homes dissipate. "Networked electronic technologies have removed any limit to what can be done in bed," Colomina contin-ues, concluding (as if relegating us to the isolating expanses of a digital desert) that "new media turns us all into inmates, constantly under surveillance, even as we celebrate endless connectivity."[5] Though none of the objects in the show featured the interactive touch screens or internet-connectivity capa-bilities one finds in the latest home appliances, all of them were produced through some sort of digital means. At the cen-ter of the exhibition was a bed, a ritual place of rest where we are confronted with the contemporary need to be always on, therefore awake. Made from a grid of welded wire mesh coated with ChromaFlair iridescent paint, *4 Poster Bed*, by RO/LU, has the spatial demeanor of Sol LeWitt's boxes or Superstudio's *Continuous Monument*—a sense that space flows in structured yet unimpeded ways, an effect amplified by the gridded canopy's mirrored ceiling.

Nature and artifice, individuals and their surroundings, are in communion in ways that seem to bypass the critiques of Colomina and Crary. In any case, for many environmental philosophers today the nature-and-artifice duality is itself artificial and not particularly useful for forging ways ahead. What surrounds

ig Mies van der Rohe, *Die Wohnung unserer Zeit*,
utsche Bauausstellung Berlin, 1931

Le Corbusier, *Pavillon de l'Esprit Nouveau*, Paris, 1925

us, whether mechanized objects or trees, valleys, and sunsets, exists equally within what we call our environment. Even without a greenscreen, the great outdoors *is* the great indoors. We constantly need to reassess the way we engage with what surrounds us. As our environment changes, so does the anonymous history, which needs to be rewritten. "We must establish a new balance between the individual and collective spheres," Giedion exhorted at the end of *Mechanization Takes Command*. "There is no static equilibrium between man and his environment, between inner and outer reality."[6] In other words, what we design around us are attempts to model larger, even global, systems. In that sense, according to Giedion, Le Corbusier's original pavilion design was not just his protest against design as decoration; the components of its interior—each table, vase, chair, or carpet—were words that could recombine into new sentences. It was at the *Pavillon de l'Esprit Nouveau*, conceived as a whole, that one first saw the interplay of heterogeneous elements "clearly and consistently expressed," Giedion stated.[7] And as if bestowing on furniture and household items a larger, connected sense of purpose, he concluded it was "time that we become human again and let the human scale rule over all our ventures."[8]

Notes

1. Sigfried Giedion, *Mechanization Takes Command: A Contribution to Anonymous History* (Oxford University Press, 1948), 620.

2. Giedion, 717.

3. Giedion, 714.

4. Beatriz Colomina, *The Century of the Bed* (Vienna: Verlag für moderne Kunst, 2014), 19.

5. Colomina, 22.

6. Giedion, *Mechanization Takes Command*, 720.

7. Giedion, 499.

8. Giedion, 723.

PAVILLON DE L'ESPRIT NOUVEAU:
A 21st Century Show Home

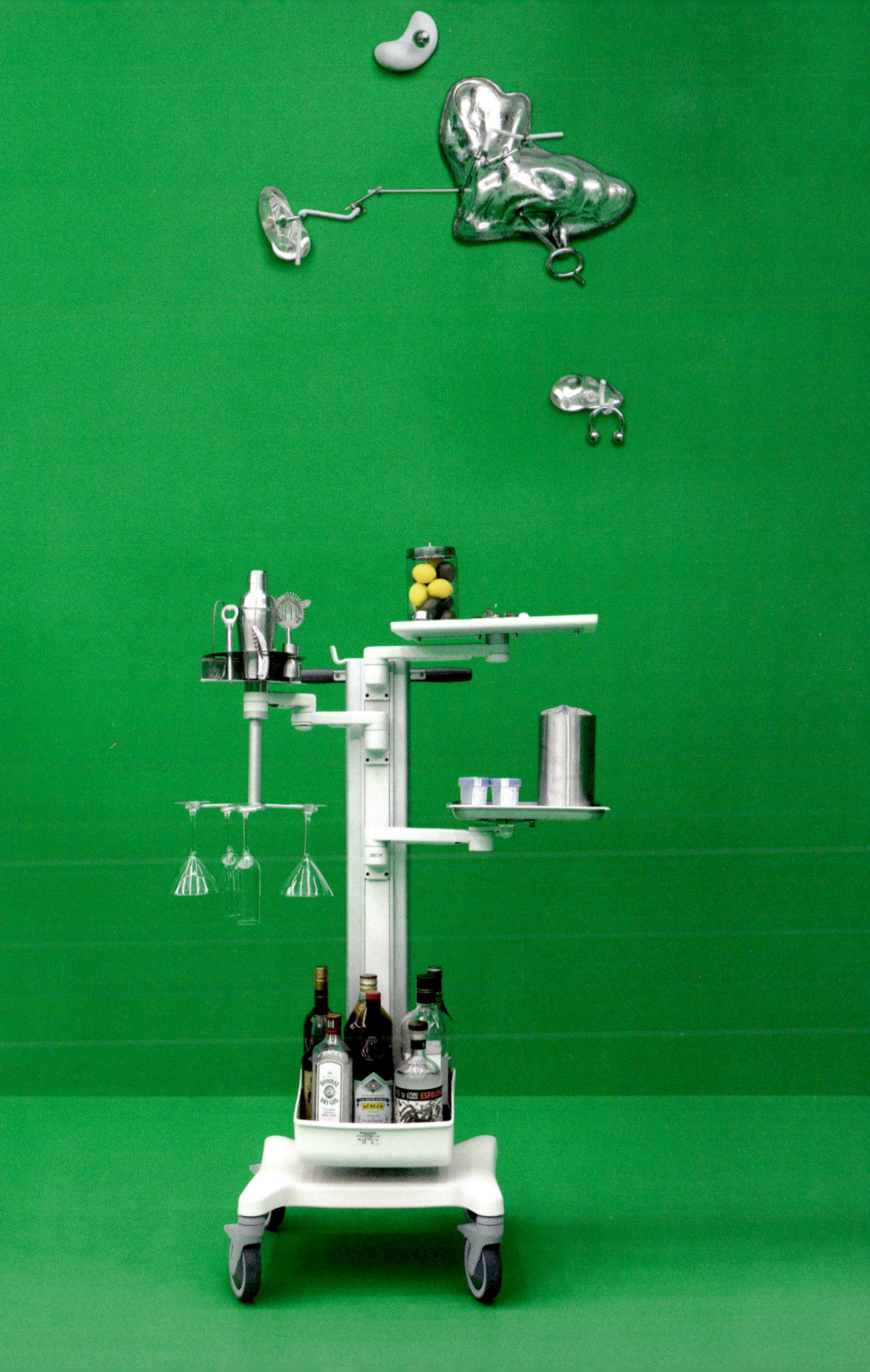

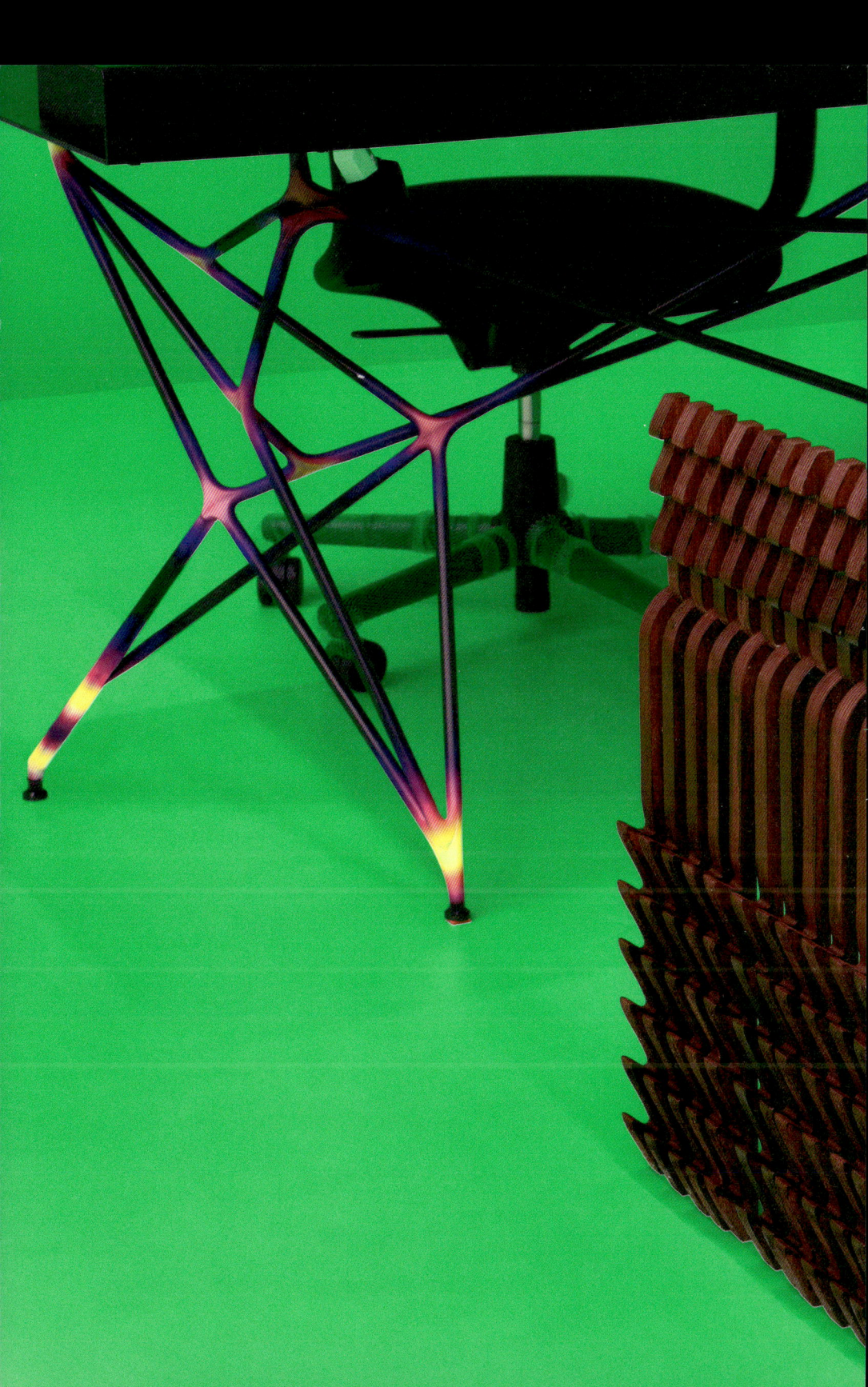

Going Green

Shawn Maximo

When Felix Burrichter and I began the exhibition design for
PAVILLON DE L'ESPRIT NOUVEAU: A 21st Century Show Home, we
initially thought about staging vignettes—framed positions and
sculptural elements within the Swiss Institute space itself.
But as we went further, we realized the answer was something
less limited and more tangible. We wanted to create the experience of actually *being in* a house while considering how domestic spaces might develop in the future. In show homes globally,
open-space plans are the driving force among many real estate
agents. These homes are all about open environments that you
can customize to your own desires. In this sense everyone can
be their own architect. Given that, it made a lot of sense
for us to make a huge, open environment, which then could be
parceled out depending on your experience and your trajectory
through the space.

We also wanted to see if we could imagine a scenario and an
organization of space that was not something totally familiar.
While so many technological advances are happening—like the
"internet of things," where all appliances can talk to one
another—many of us still live in old houses and still cherish
the ability to live in old homes with "character." And so this
exhibition was an opportunity to blow that open and say, "Well,
we're only fifteen years into this century, what are people
going to be doing in eighty years? What will 'character' mean
at that moment in time?" I don't know anyone with a greenscreen
house yet, but a greenscreen allows you to inhabit and project
different environments and realities onto your space. The greenscreen home is the open plan taken to the next level, producing
a whole different type of openness. I thought of the moment
in the television show *The Comeback* when the main character,
Valerie Cherish, goes into a huge bulbous space that's entirely
green. She practically disappears into this totalizing greenscreen world.

Le Corbusier himself spoke on the necessity of tools—underscoring
how tools really represent the contemporary state of affairs
because tools are good only as long as they're useful. Once a
tool's no longer useful, you throw it away. As Le Corbusier
put it:

We throw the out-of-date tool on the scrap-heap: the car-
bine, the culverin, the growler and the old locomotive.
This action is a manifestation of health, of moral health,
of *morale* also; it is not right that we should produce bad
things because of a bad tool; nor is it right that we should
waste our energy, our health, and our courage because of a
bad tool; it must be thrown away and replaced. But men live
in old houses and they have not yet thought of building
houses adapted to themselves.[1]

This was a show home that adapted to and was adapted for not
just one inhabitant but a plurality of possible residents.
It displayed the tools for making a life for the twenty-first
century. Thus, the spaces we imagined and rendered for this
show home were necessarily hybrid. They were about imagining
how people will live in the future, how they'll draw boundaries
or fail to differentiate between their kitchens and bedrooms,
between the indoors and outdoors, between nostalgic chrome-
plated spit-roasting and tactical meal replacements. Radical
hybridity has already come to define our world and experiences
at the outset of this century. This show home served as a contemporary snapshot of where things are going. The images we
created for the exhibition are often uncanny and show a future
that for some might be exciting or for others might
feel vaguely dystopian.

The living room, or Soft Surrender Lounge, served as a reminder
of this. It forced us to confront the role energy plays in our
lives and imagine a point in human, urban evolution where the
energy landscape necessary to power our lives begins to surround us, but it imagined this in a positive, even appealing,
way. It's a space where you can arrive and feel relaxed, and
simply enjoy this new post-natural environment.

The dining room, or Communal Soul Collation Center, further
highlighted the state where the boundaries between natural and
human-made elements become more ambiguous. It was inspired by a
trip I took to Bear Mountain State Park, ostensibly a natural
oasis of sorts, about forty miles from New York City. In reality,
it's a hybrid space, packed with cars and roads and people bar-
becuing. People "escape" to a nature preserve, yet they still
bring urban life with them. In the future people will probably
still be bringing their barbecues out into the so-called wild,
wherever that is, and maybe, eventually, will even incorporate
them directly into their domestic space. Having walls that open
to become cooking elements stems from this notion. The exhibition imagined what a room would look like if you were to open
the hearth and actually be able to watch as your walls cook
your food. It removes the superstructure of the oven to make
the entire room itself into an oven.

This show home depicted a future that connects us even more, and by doing so not only shows us the hope of sharing with others but also exposes us to the dark side of humanity. This tension is something that we have to coexist with. While none of these speculative environments go to the dark side per se, many took advantage of a sort of ambivalence or ambiguity. For example, the bedroom, the Temple of Dreams: Is it for sleeping or working, nighttime adult S & M activities or daytime childcare? Can't it be and maybe isn't it already all the above? Even the garden, the Serenity Gateway, conceived a new future relationship to plants—a weed garden, where the plants we normally dispose of take center stage and psychedelic flora sprouts up. It was a decidedly untraditional type of garden.

These seemingly basic questions that we face daily will only increase as the century progresses, further eroding clear boundaries and hybridizing our living spaces. How will the aesthetics and materials of medical equipment and the atmosphere of the hospital affect how we live and what objects we live with? What is it to be on-screen and under watch? All these tensions that were below the surface will come to a head as our lifestyle in the twenty-first century continues to radically evolve.

Notes

1.   Le Corbusier, *Toward a New Architecture* (London: Architectural Press, 1965), 13.

Index

Text by Marc Matchak

Shawn Maximo
Serenity Gateway, 2015
Looping HD video animation

For *PDLEN* Shawn Maximo, with Filip Setmanuk, created digital
environments displayed on flat greenscreen monitors, with the
furniture in the various rooms keyed into the animation. With
the use of cameras and chroma-key compositing backgrounds,
viewers were projected into these environments, each one softly
delineating the exhibition's six zones. The first animation,
Serenity Gateway, consisted of a digital rendering of a cul-
tivated weed garden of psychedelic plants such as peyote. It
also contained a spiral stairway reminiscent of the courtyard
stairs in Le Corbusier's 1925 *Pavillon de L'Esprit Nouveau* that
descended into an unknown underground space.

Camille Blin
Gradient, 2009
Milled aluminum, LED light, printed glass

Camille Blin's *Gradient* lamp merges the function of a light
dimmer—typically a hidden electrical component—into the form
of a lampshade. The lamp itself is composed of a minimal aluminum body and a graphic gradient silk-screened onto a glass disc
that shifts from opaque black to completely translucent. The
lampshade, which can be spun in front of a light source, distributes light of varying intensity, allowing users to control
the transition from light to dark.

Piero Lissoni/Paul Kopkau
Carbon Frog, 2015
Carbon fiber, plastic, polyester cord

When the designer Piero Lissoni first crafted this chair in
1995, it was known simply as *Frog*. Twenty years later he
updated it, replacing the metal legs with carbon fiber and the
seat with interwoven polyester cord. This ultra-light, ultra-
relaxing chair is known as *Carbon Frog*. In yet another modifi-
cation for *PDLEN,* the artist Paul Kopkau affixed plastic pipes
to the legs to mutate it into a rocking chair. Lissoni's high-
tech materials contrast with Kopkau's decidedly low-tech elements, like plastic pipes found in stores for DIY home-improve-
ment supplies, creating a cunning allegory for the creeping
infiltration of scientific advances into the most mundane
domestic settings.

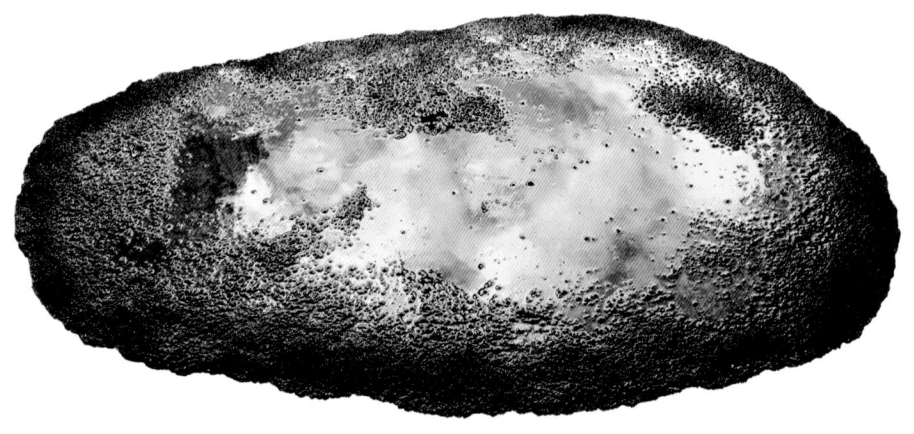

Marlie Mul
Puddle (Faint Green), 2014
Puddle (Small Twig), 2013
Sand, resin

Marlie Mul makes lifelike "puddles" out of stones, sand, resin,
and other found ephemera. These floor sculptures mimic the
quotidian experience of suddenly encountering a puddle on the
street. When transposed into the *PDLEN* exhibition space, which
simulated a garden, Mul's works took on a meta-level that spoke
to the hybrid nature of the contemporary city, between what is
authentic or gentrified and what is real or virtual.

Studio Drift
Fragile Future 3.13, 2013
Dandelion seeds, phosphorus bronze, LEDs, Perspex

In an attempt to develop a radical new design language at
the intersection of nature and technology, Studio Drift, an
Amsterdam-based collective founded by Lonneke Gordijn and
Ralph Nauta, questions how these seemingly disparate worlds can
merge and evolve. They incorporated dandelion seeds in *Fragile
Future*, a modular light system that can grow and extend, adapt-
ing to its context in endless variations, much as dandelions
spread rapidly wherever they are planted. After being hand-
picked and dried, each dandelion seed is meticulously connected
to an LED light.

Shawn Maximo
Soft Surrender Lounge, 2015
Looping HD video animation

In the animation for *PDLEN*'s living-room setting, Maximo, with
Filip Setmanuk, imagined a future in which the energy landscape
is an inescapable part of the domestic environment. Homes currently camouflage or hide their sources of energy and power,
but in *Soft Surrender Lounge* the energy sources were ever present, in a desert environment featuring a concrete platform sur-
rounded by columns supporting wind turbines and solar panels.

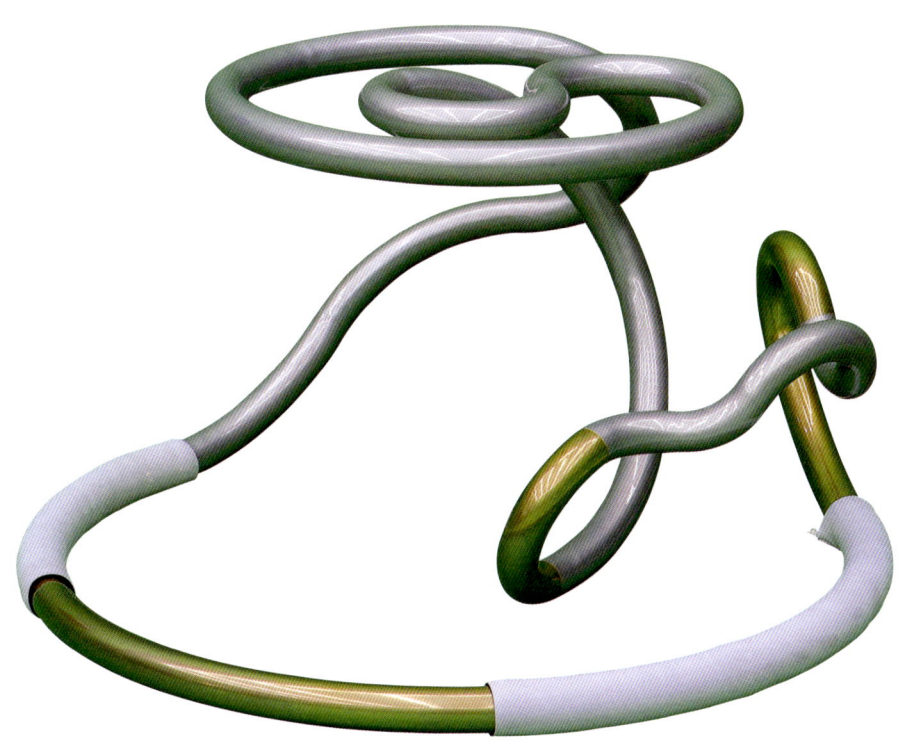

Aranda\Lasch
Railing Lounge Chair, 2015
Railing Stool, 2015
Polished stainless steel, fabric and foam upholstery

Aranda\Lasch's *Railing Lounge Chair* and *Railing Stool* further
the duo's development of a radical, modular language in furniture. Commissioned for the exhibition, each piece is made from
one line, with a single set of off-the-shelf steel arcs connected to form a continuous loop. For comfort, the designers
wrapped the "seat" of each object in silicone foam, suggesting
invisible arms possessed by a spongey grip. Both pieces formal-
ly appear much like an ouroboros, having no start or end point,
highlighting how self-consumption is a necessity for the furniture of the future.

Hélène Dashorst
Mimic, 2015
Phthalate-free vinyl

Both textiles capture the
multifunctional aspect of
throw pillows as a furnish-
ing both decorative and useful
for comfort almost anywhere
in the domestic environ-
ment. Commissioned to design
a textile for *PDLEN*, Hélène
Dashorst worked with Designtex
to create a fabric optimized
for function and durability in
high-traffic areas. Since the
fabric was designed for use
not just in the home but for
the outdoors and travel, its
pairing with the throw pillows
emphasized themes of mobility,
proving *Mimic* to be elegant
yet enduring.

Designtex
Flip, 2015
Polyurethane

Committed to exploring the
interaction of light and color
in textile design, Designtex
mixed light-interference pigment with conventional dyes
to create a complex surface.
Flip, a polyurethane textile
woven through with flakes of
interference pigments, colors
the yarn and acts as a re-
fracting prism. Much like a
holographic surface, the fabric shifts its color depending
on the viewer's perspective.

Max Lamb
Marmoreal Low Table, 2015
Marmoreal black engineered marble

For *PDLEN* Max Lamb designed a monumental coffee table with
large, colorful chunks fitting neatly within its distinctive
surface. The process of making *Marmoreal Low Table* combined
engineered marble cast into ten-metric-ton blocks, milled or
cut into slabs with dimension-quarrying waste materials and a
polyester resin, resulting in minimal environmental impact. The
terrazzo surface and plinth-like shape combine to form a contemporary table that, like its ancient predecessors, is strong
enough to endure time.

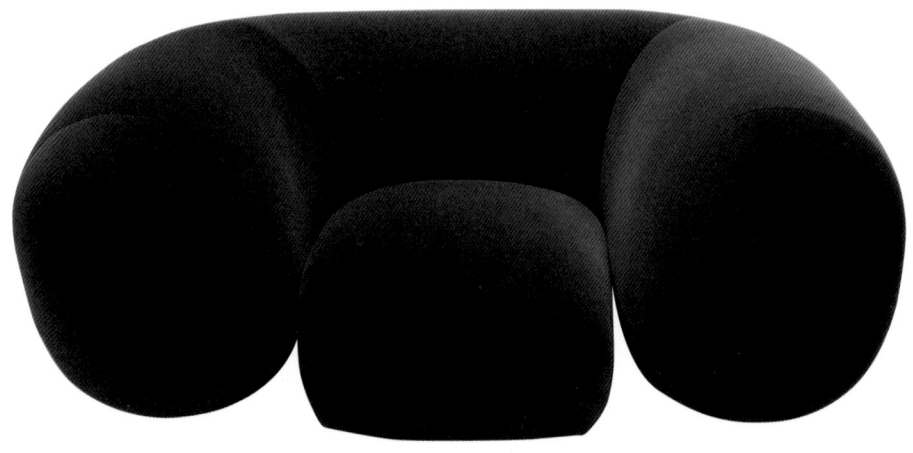

Philippe Malouin
Mollo, 2014
Polystyrene foam, stretch velvet

Phillipe Malouin's *Mollo* chair has no internal structure. It is
made using only polystyrene foam and stretch velvet, a blend of
wool and synthetics that allows for upholstery without creases
or wrinkles. The chair's continuous form is mapped by an exag-
gerated stitch detailing that outlines the seat, arms, and
backrest. Its oversize shape challenges convention by accom-
modating seating on all four of its sides. With an adaptability
similar to that of app-based technology, *Mollo* beckons the sit-
ter from any number of angles.

Jonathan Muecke
CS (Coiled Stool), 2013
Carbon and aramid fibers, epoxy, resin

Following the lineage of research in composite tubular struc-
tures, *CS (Coiled Stool)* is made from a single tube of carbon
and aramid fibers coiled into a mold and fixed under pressure with epoxy resin. Unlike its precedents—Michael Thonet's
bentwood pieces and Le Corbusier's bent-steel chairs—Jonathan
Muecke's stool harmonizes structure and surface in a seam-
less singular integration, without nuts and bolts, totally
hardware-free.

Jessi Reaves
I just live here, 2015
Plyboo, polyurethane foam, studio dust, adhesive, oriented
strand board, cedar, linen, Lycra, polar fleece, glass, ink,
hardware

Like Kopkau's intervention in Lissoni's *Carbon Frog*, Jessi
Reaves's *I just live here* sofa subverts the neat, packaged con-
notations of the familiar household object. It emphasizes the
necessity of engineered wood for domestic furniture, a development that became common at the start of the twentieth century.
Exposing the "messy" frame and using a range of composite woods
like Plyboo, oriented strand board, and homemade particleboard,
Reaves reveals the intrinsic beauty in the mundanity of furniture production.

Christian Wassmann
Red, Yellow, and Blue Dodecahedron, 2015
Polyurethane resin

Christian Wassmann's *Red, Yellow, and Blue Dodecahedron*, a
chandelier and optical instrument, is an homage to the incan-
descent light bulb at the core of optical light and a study of
how light shapes color. Its pentagon-shaped polyurethane lenses
are tinted with the three primary pigment colors and have been
adjoined to form a dodecahedron, one of the five Platonic sol-
ids. Inside is an upside-down reflection of the chandelier's
surroundings, bearing the entirety of the color spectrum and
revealing the environment's dependence on light.

Shawn Maximo
Communal Soul Collation Center, 2015
Looping HD video animation

Playing to the extremes of the automated home, *Communal Soul
Collation Center* simulated the futuristic experience of cooking
and dining inside an open-air oven. By creating a slightly dystopian space to eat in, Maximo, with Filip Setmanuk, revealed
how ritual domestic activities will come to shape the architecture where food is prepared and consumed.

Laureline Galliot
LUCKY TOAD, 2012
3-D printed mold, colored powder

As an alternative to conventional wireframe virtual models
used for 3-D printing, Laureline Galliot developed an intuitive
modeling process that emphasizes dimensionality. Much like the
futurist works of Henri Gaudier-Brzeska, Galliot's sculptural
vase sits somewhere between a figurative and abstract realiza-
tion, resuming the conversation between nature and mankind's
distortion of nature through mechanized processes. Focusing on
mass rather than line allows her to effectively turn colors
into physical objects.

Katie Stout
Lip Placemats, 2015
Rope and terry cloth treated with Nanotex

Like much of the designer's work, Katie Stout's *Lip Placemats*
toe the line between play and function. The shapes are achieved
by sewing synthetic rope together in a process similar to
braiding rugs. Although hung on the wall of the Communal Soul
Collation Center, the combined placemats and napkins were
intended for table use. In fact, the lips seem to situate themselves as a sort of reflecting pool for whoever is eating. The
tongue-shaped napkins were fabricated from Nanotex, a fabric
that has been altered using nanotechnology to make it stain-
and water-resistant.

Bethan Laura Wood
Moon Rock-Dinner, 2015
Polished MDF, laser-cut hand-placed laminate marquetry,
four-leaf CNC-cut extension ring in MDF, black laminate,
powder-coated steel legs

Inspired by the moon's crater-filled landscape and the dream-
like compositions of the solar system, Bethan Laura Wood's
Moon Rock series was produced by combining classic marquetry
techniques with contemporary laser-cutting technology. Playing
with themes of exploration and space, *Moon Rock-Dinner* acknowledges the dining table as a territory for new ideas and unbound
conversation.

Joris Laarman
Makerchair (Diamond), 2014
Black and white maple

Joris Laarman's *Maker* series represents a synthesis of parametric design, digital fabrication, and traditional handcraft.
Each chair, including the *Makerchair (Diamond)*, is an amalga-
mation of wooden parts engineered with precision to fit like
a three-dimensional puzzle. Building a whole out of so many
small elements allows for greater complexity of form, modulated
smoothly, in a way that seems organic. Placed strategically in
the Communal Soul Collation Center, these chairs, though fabricated through inorganic mechanization, appeared natural in the
sense that they were sprung from the environment.

Soft Baroque
Desktop Furniture, 2015
Powder-coated aluminum, light-absorbent material

Pushing the boundaries between spectacle and function in design, Saša Štucin and Nicholas Gardner of Soft Baroque explore
the complexity in digital representation. Commissioned for the
exhibition, *Desktop Furniture* exists in both a physical and
digital world. The shelf, made of thin, powder-coated aluminum,
has faces coated with a light-absorbent material, rendering it
"hollow." The result was an optical illusion where the physical
object attempts to flatten itself into a digital image. Concur-
rent with its place in the realm of the exhibition, the piece
was also available as a downloadable digital image file—a visual device to help organize a computer desktop.

Jasper Morrison
Alfi, 2015
Reclaimed post-industrial waste, polypropylene, wood fiber,
ash wood

Jasper Morrison's *Alfi* chair was inspired by the woven-cane
chairs that are ubiquitous in Paris. Its seat is made from
wood-filled reclaimed polypropylene, a subset of natural fiber
plastic composites, combined with a base of harvested ash wood
handcrafted by Amish woodworkers. For *PDLEN* the chair's base
was painted chroma-key green, making it appear to float in
space when projected onto the greenscreen.

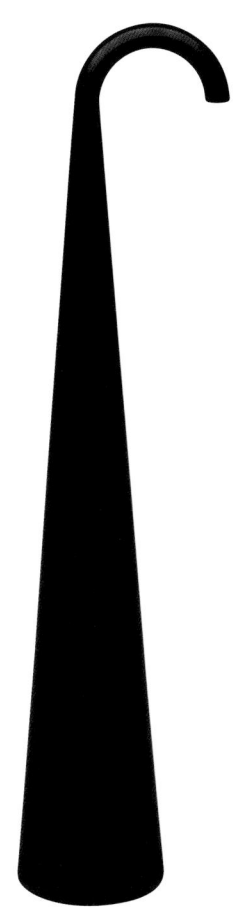

Leon Ransmeier
Cane, 2015
3-D printed nylon

Leon Ransmeier's prototype for a cane exemplifies industrial
design's humanistic potency for a changing demographic. The
sturdy, ultra-light 3-D printed nylon cane offers its compan-
ionship to busy people on the go while also proving to be a
versatile design object of contemplation. Themes of comfort and
reliability are instilled in the cartoonish shape of the cane,
realized with sculptural potential for the space of the living
room.

Patricia Urquiola
Serena, 2015
LED, aluminum, photo-engraved polymethyl methacrylate

Patricia Urquiola's *Serena* lamp is characterized by its ovular
form, evoking the shape of a metallic leaf or the pistil of a
flower. The light source is outfitted with a dimmable LED while
the reflector is made from sheared and folded pre-anodized
aluminum. The fleeting figure of the leaf exemplifies state-of-
the-art LED technology, which only a few years ago was expen-
sive and reserved largely for industrial use.

Shawn Maximo
Synergy Station, 2015
Looping HD video animation

Maximo believes that in the future, stored information will
be increasingly visible. With Filip Setmanuk he created the
Synergy Station, a room that paired the archival aspect of a
server space with the cathartic environment of the gym, placing objects for physical fitness within the master brain of a
vast computer network. The animation unified the two functions
within a single living environment.

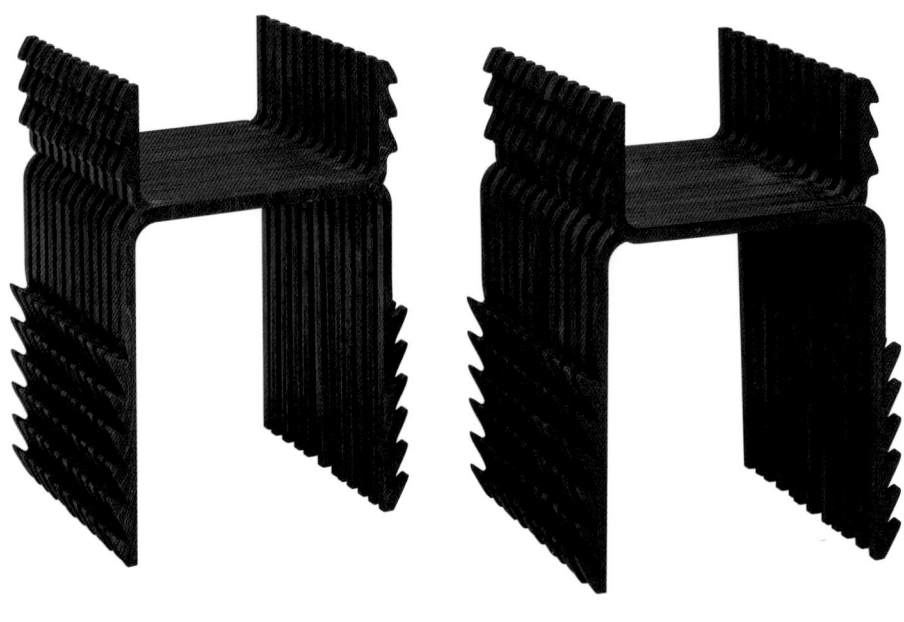

Alessandro Bava
LES Chair, 2015
CNC-milled stained plywood and stainless-steel rod

The prototype for the *LES Chair* is the latest piece from a
series in which Alessandro Bava explores the form of the *sella
curulis*, an ancient Roman stool that was a symbol of imperial
power. In a nod to the stool's status in antiquity, the title
cheekily acknowledges New York City's Lower East Side neighbor-
hood as a longstanding place of cultural gatekeeping, a hotbed
for career climbing and social capital. Bava's version of the
stool was made with a CNC machine using a CAD proportional system for parametric transformations and features a simple construction method—a repeating X that distributes loads and guar-
antees easy assemblage.

Josh Bitelli
Once Is Never, 2015
Silvered glass, chromed steel fixings, powder-coated architectural iron, anodized aluminum, stainless-steel medical
external-fixation device, acrylic-sprayed plaster resin

In this work by the artist Josh Bitelli, gnarled rock-climbing
holds seem to have crawled onto the gallery walls all on their
own. The collection of incised materials and appendages that
compose *Once Is Never* work to create a conceptual trifecta of
medical support devices, body ornaments, and human reflection,
suggesting a potent mirror image of the ever-increasing pursuit
of human physical perfection. Not quite suitable for either a
medical office or a piercing salon, *Once Is Never* evokes a per-
version of form and function in the space of the exhibition.

79

Josh Bitelli
Outsized Nutrition, 2015
Porcelain cast in soft white loaf

In his *Outsized Nutrition* series, Bitelli creates trophies
made out of bread molds. The work stems from a long-standing
tradition among bread factories, where extra-large loaves were
made alongside the normal-sized ones, then carved out and used
as molds for casting porcelain, as a kind of second baking.
The emulsified and chemically treated bread leaves a trace in
the original mold, glazing the ceramics with a sugary, iridescent skin. *Outsized Nutrition* conflates a symbol of suste-
nance with ideas about population growth and infrastructures of
production.

Nicoletta Rossi and Guido Bianchi
Ipnos, 2014
Anodized aluminum, LED light

This redesign of a traditional floor lamp is made of a light-
weight and minimalist aluminum skeleton. At first glance *Ipnos*
seems to be just a structure, yet it duplicitously functions
with a soft light emission. The frame is embedded with small
LED lights within the upper edge of the hollow volume, a detail
that creates an illumination of the surrounding space. Rossi
and Bianchi crafted the indoor-outdoor floor lamp with concise
parameters, while leaving the possibility of turning it into a
small table by placing a transparent methacrylate panel on top.

Konstantin Grcic
Allstar, 2015
Polyamide, steel

Through its shape, both inviting and simple, Konstantin Grcic's
Allstar office chair challenges contemporary corporate aesthetics. While still incorporating the most important functions—a
swivel base, an adjustable synchronized mechanism, seat depth,
height adjustment, and an adjustable backrest—Grcic opts for
customization, offering a number of colors and combinations.
By doing so, he responds to the twenty-first century's mobile,
personalized work culture, where fixed desks at a 9-to-5 office
space have become outmoded.

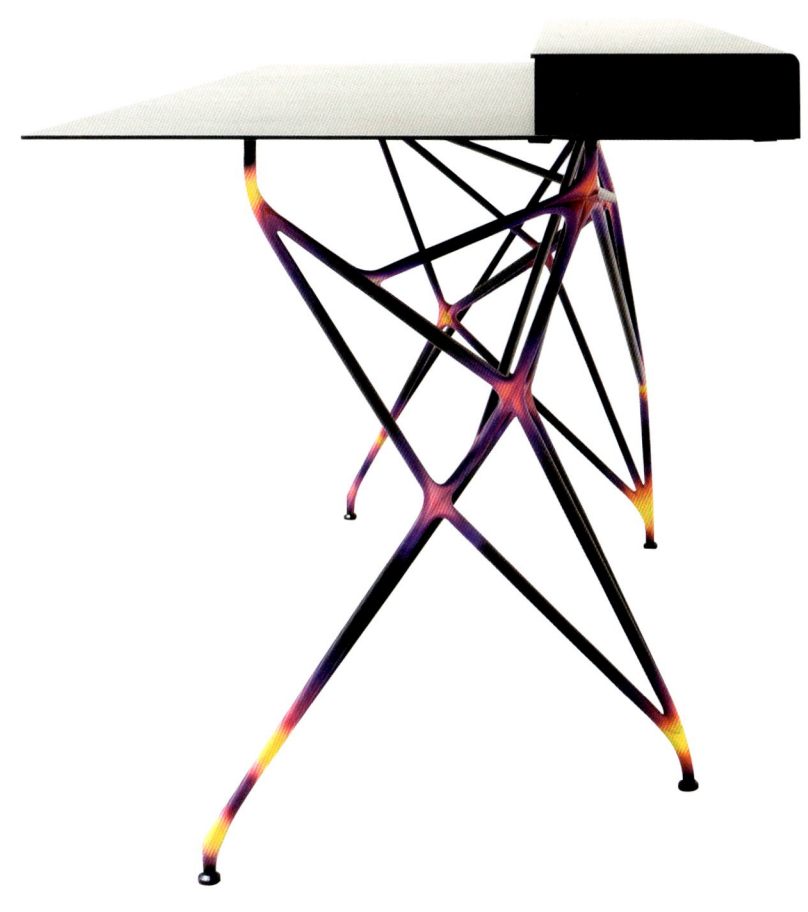

Kram/Weisshaar
MULTITHREAD #03 Escritoire, 2012
3-D printed aluminium joints, high tensile strength steel tube,
powder coated aluminium table top.

This small writing desk in the design duo Reed Kram and Clemens
Weisshaar's *MULTITHREAD* series begins simply with a network of
thin bars positioned to support a horizontal surface in space.
The structure then goes through software developed by the designers, using algorithms and finite element analysis to visu-
alize all the forces passing through the piece. The software
outputs a representation of the loads acting on the structure—
made of steel tubes and aluminum joints 3-D printed through a
process known as selective laser melting (SLM)—which is painted
onto the structural frame, illustrating an energy ever-present
in design innovation.

Shawn Maximo
Sarco, 2014
Sapele wood, plastic marble laminate, steel shelving, dichroic
glass

Maximo's *Sarco* shelving units are hand-assembled from a para-
doxical mix of mechanized and organic components: sapele wood
veneer sourced from tropical Africa, plastic marble high-pres-
sure laminate, and standard metal shelving devices. Together
with custom-fabricated dichroic glass shelves, *Sarco* consti-
tutes a Frankenstein's monster through globalized exchange,
combining to near overload many of the material trends found in
the gym/office of the future.

Laureline Galliot
MASK, 2012
3-D printed mold, various colored powders

Galliot combines images of her past and present selves through
digital animation rendering software, which she discovered
while working for Disney. For *MASK*, she collected photographs
of herself to create a double-sided self-portrait: the front of
the mask represents her adult face, while the inside depicts
her as a young child. Methodically redeveloping the same identity, Galliot sculpts and paints the object virtually with this
technology before printing its colored form.

Shawn Maximo
Holistic Support Zone, 2015
Looping HD video animation

In providing a luxurious, environmentally friendly place for
people to do their business, Maximo created, with Filip Setmanuk, the *Holistic Support Zone*, a space which acknowledged the
circular process of waste disposal, growth, and consumption.
Instead of hiding the act of excretion in a separate room, the
zone emphasized it by having it occur in a vast area featuring
marble floors and walls, a handwoven rug, and a small garden.

Ifeanyi Oganwu
BULGY Inverted, 2014
Stainless steel

Ifeanyi Oganwu's mind-bending shelf structure uses mirror-
polished stainless steel to blur the distinction between interior
and exterior, structure and surface. The planar shelves form a
substructure intersecting a dramatic, draped curving surface.
The surfaces, which measure only 3 mm thick, interlock like
traditional wood joints, with laser-cut slots and machined
grooves holding up the assembly with the help of minimal spot
welds. For the exhibition, *BULGY Inverted* functioned essentially
as a kitchen counter for the Holistic Support Zone, presenting
the various flavors of Sean Raspet's Soylent concoctions.

Sean Raspet
CCCCC1CCC(=O)O1, CCCCCCC1CCC(=O)O1 CCCCCCCCC1CCC(=O)O1
CCCC1CCCC(=O)O1 CCCCCC1CCCC(=O)O1 CCCCCCCC1CCCC(=O)O1
(Technical Milk), 2015
Gamma-octalactone, gamma-decalactone,
gamma-dodecalactone, delta-octalactone, delta-decalactone,
delta-dodecalactone, provided at approximately 0.1% in Soylent™
vehicle

CC1=CC=CC(C)=N1 CCC1=CN=C(C=C1)C CCC1=CN=CC=C1
CC1C(=O)C(=C(O1)C)O CCC1C(=O)C(=C(O1)C)O
(Technical Food), 2015
2,6-dimethylpyridine, 3-ethylpyridine, 5-ethyl-2-methylpyri-
dine, furaneol, homofuraneol, provided at approximately 0.1% in
Soylent™ vehicle

For *PDLEN* the artist Sean Raspet created two flavors of the
nutritional solution Soylent™. In its original conception,
Soylent™ contains a blank or nondescript flavor, part of its
inventor's goal of breaking food down into its essential nu-
trients. Introducing a slight dimensionality to the concoc-
tion, the flavors of *Technical Milk* and *Technical Food* were the
result of Raspet's abstracting a myriad of existing molecules
found in food and milk into small sets of analogous molecules—a
synthetic "food in general" and "milk in general" flavor, con-
densed and simplified.

Nanu Al-Hamad
Med-Bar, 2015
Medical-grade steel and plastic, bar accessories, alcohol

Using the variable height-mounting solution for medical carts
to radically reimagine the wet bar, Nanu Al-Hamad flushed the
vitality of medical equipment into a conceptual sculpture. The
designer's appropriation suggested that the cocktail is a form
of twenty-first-century medicine. *Med-Bar* foreshadows the domestic setting of the future, one that is not merely furnished
but adapted to the homeowner's health. The interior will be
continuously subjected to the changing abilities of the occupant, whether from addiction or the necessity of home care.

Shawn Maximo
Temple of Dreams, 2015
Looping HD video animation

Using the ominous image of a concrete submarine bunker, Maximo,
with Filip Setmanuk, created this animation which imagined that
in the future the most intimate space in the domestic environment would be subject to constant scrutiny. Suggestive of alien
forms, *Temple of Dreams* positioned aquatic life hovering above
the bedroom's glass ceiling as a living surveillance system
while cameras record continuously, acknowledging the increasing
unattainability of a truly personal space, even in the bedroom.

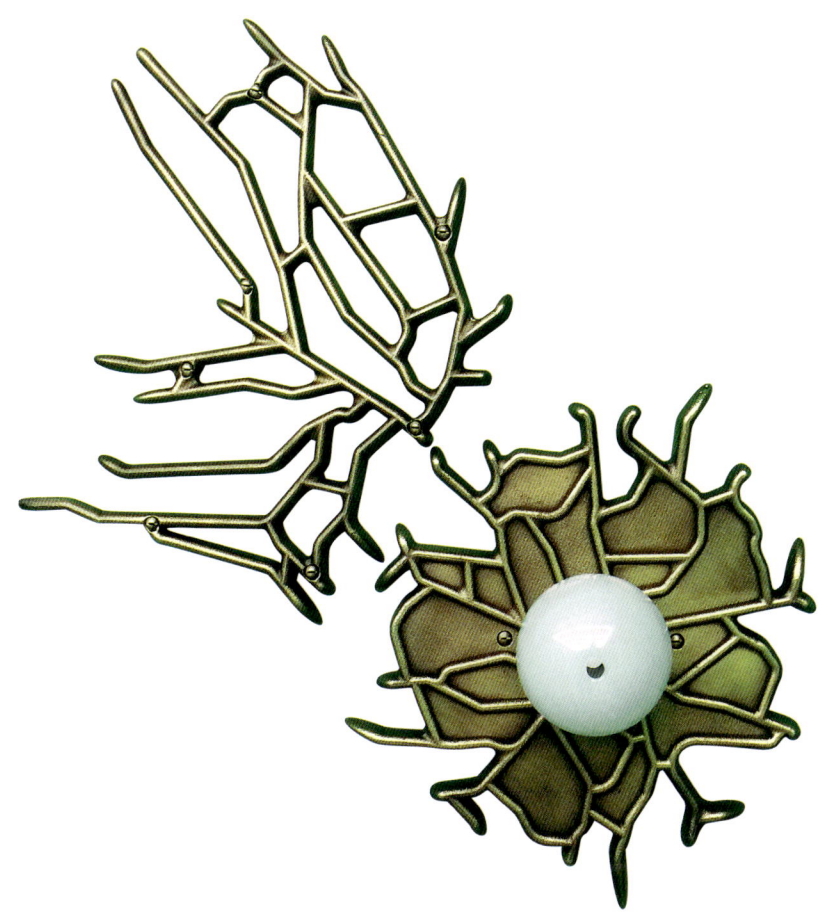

Lindsey Adelman
Marina, 2015
Brass plated polymer

Lindsey Adelman's studio explores the aesthetic parallels
between the natural world and industrialization. Her sculptural lighting compositions, exemplified by the *Marina* lighting series, manifest the wandering, organic growth of a natural
process realized by technological refinement. The sconces commissioned for the exhibition were made with a combination of
3-D printing, brass plating, and glassblowing, realized through
the precision of a machine-led manufacturing process.

Konstantin Grcic
Emboss, 2015
Polyurethane

Grcic, with the aid of the commercial manufacturer Maharam,
developed a new way of embossing polyurethane. The non-woven
textile is covered in a tactile, gridded pattern of clustered
dots that vary in size and depth. While the fabric's lus-
trous surface has the appearance of a moon-like landscape, the
abstract print was actually inspired by a surface detail the
designer saw on a piece of factory machinery. Mechanization
and organic other-worldliness intersect to create a futuristic
cover for RO/LU's *Four Poster Bed*.

RO/LU
Four Poster Bed, 2015
Welded steel mesh, ChromaFlair paint, mirror

A furniture type dating back to the sixteenth century is cast
into the twenty-first with the characteristic minimalism of
Matt Olson and Mike Brady, the co-founders of RO/LU. *Four
Poster Bed* consists of welded wire mesh coated with ChromaFlair
paint to impart an iridescent quality to its edges. The canopy
is outfitted with a full-size mirror so that the users of the
bed can see themselves merge with objects, or people, they love.

Felix Burrichter and Shawn Maximo
TV Stand, 2015
Chrome, brass, dichroic glass

Composed of the same core elements as the USM Haller System—
ball joints, connecting tubes, and panel inserts—but with a
rather different material palette, the collaboration between
Felix Burrichter and Shawn Maximo for *PDLEN* was an evolution
of USM's modular furniture system, originally developed in the
1960s by the Swiss architect Fritz Haller. This TV table for-
goes USM's chrome balls and minimalist metal panels in favor of
unpolished brass and dichroic panels, permitting a multitude of
color reflections.

Guto Requena
Nóize, 2013
3-D printed using ABS

Guto Requena's *Nóize* chair combines a 3-D modeled *Giraffe*
chair—the 1987 piece designed by Lina Bo Bardi, Marcelo Ferraz,
and Marcelo Suzuki—with a digital sound recording of Santa
Ifigênia Street in downtown São Paulo, Requena's native city.
The *Giraffe* chair was faithfully rendered through digital mod-
elling only to be deformed by overlaying visualized data,
sourced from the audio recordings. The final 3-D printed result
was an uncanny transformation of a modernist design icon by a
patchwork of the voices, sounds, and complexities of our present moment. *Nóize* invited reflection on digital culture, bohe-
mia, authorship, and design's narrative potential.

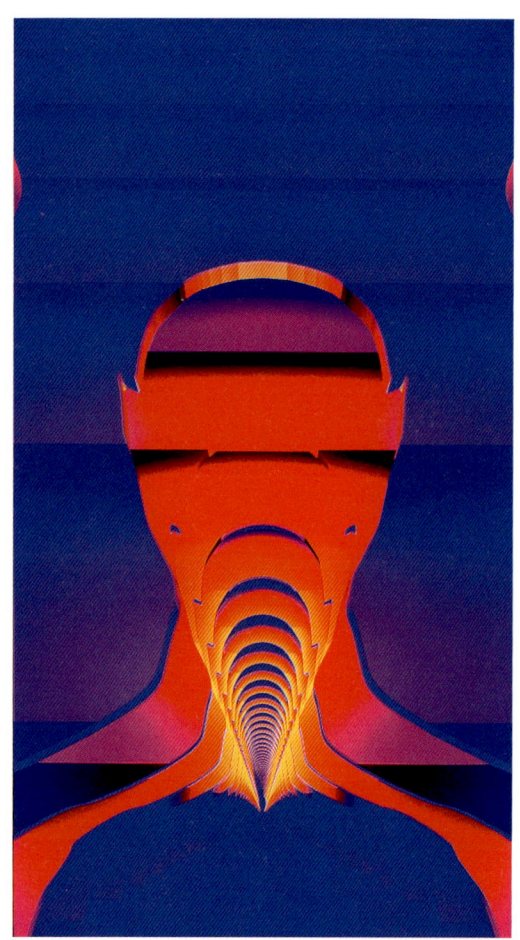

Gustavo Torres (Kidmograph)
NDLSS_MND, 2014
GIF

Positioned as a vanity mirror, Gustavo Torres's *NDLSS_MND* silhouettes and abstracts the rebounding self. In an infinite GIF
loop, expanding heads hypnotically radiate outward in a palette
of yellow, red, purple, and blue. Warping reflections of color
and impression of surrounding objects in the process of modify-
ing the viewer's own reflection, this work invites us to ques-
tion how identity is projected through domestic space.

Robert Stadler
Cut_Paste #1 (Console), 2013
Marble (Bianco Carrara, Striato Olimpo, Travertino)
and aluminum

Robert Stadler's *Cut_Paste* façades are made of marble panels of
varying sizes, each resembling the sawn-off, discarded scraps
one might find in a construction site. The designer combines
different silhouettes and grain patterns to create constructiv-
ist-inspired assemblages that appear to be the ruins of a monumental, modern architecture masquerading as domestic objects.
The panels, distinguished by their thinness, are marble-alumi-
num composites often used to save material and weight in architectural façades. Slightly calamitous, *Cut_Paste #1* regards
the enduring quality of sustainable architecture with a certain
volatility.

Ian Stell
Sidewinder, 2015
Dyed maple, white oak, brass and nylon pivots

Ian Stell's furniture is inspired by the pantograph, a six-
teenth-century instrument used for copying and scaling drawings
and texts. Comprising hundreds of dyed curly-maple and white-
oak components held together by a system of internal brass
pivots, the *Sidewinder* side table was assembled in a painstak-
ing process combining the techniques of beading, weaving, and
bridge-building. Its accordion-like structure allows it to be
activated by a simple push or pull, enabling the form to shift,
expand, or contract.

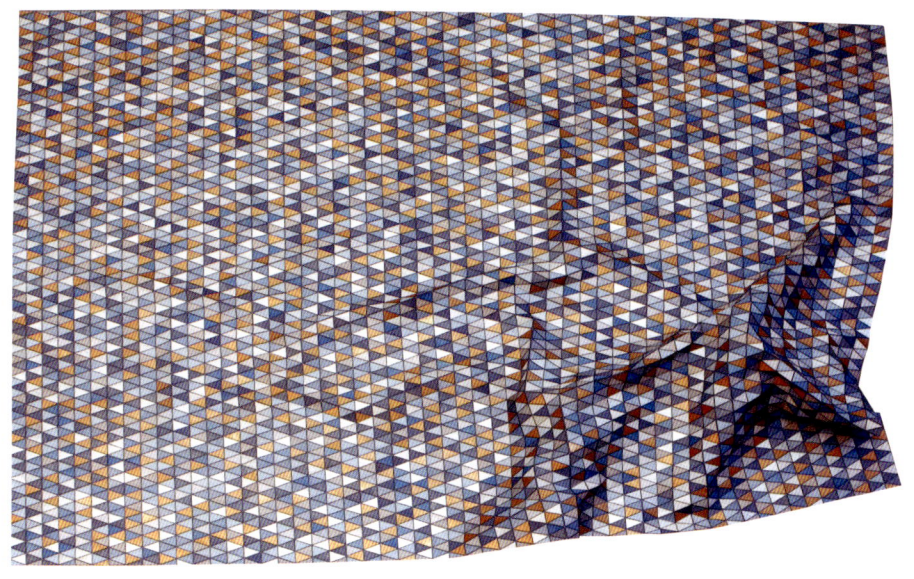

Elisa Strozyk
Reflecting Blue, 2014
Stained birch plywood, cotton

Elisa Strozyk's multifaceted *Reflecting Blue* rug is made of
thousands of triangle shapes laser-cut from wood veneer sewn
onto a fabric underlay. Its unexpected tactility offers material in flux, allowing an unrestrained potential for constant
transformation. Color further abstracts the materiality and
alludes to familiar patterns in traditional carpets. The final
object challenges what can be expected from wood in both material and function.

Julika Rudelius
Threshold, 2015
HD Video

In *Threshold*, commissioned for *PDLEN*, the artist Julika
Rudelius took viewers on a tour through the imagined homes of
two celebrities. The video—constructed from composite images,
3-D models, helicopter footage, and simulations found on the
internet, along with deliberately rudimentary projection map-
ping—reproduced the domestic settings of the mansions belonging
to Kim Kardashian and Lisa Vanderpump, whose homes double as
the locations for their respective reality TV shows. Rudelius
forged a realm of analog and digital fantasies exploring the
feedback loop of desire, inherent to the public's obsession
with semi-private spaces.

Text contribution: Alexandra Alexa

Public Programs

Conversation
Going Green: Felix Burrichter
and Shawn Maximo in
conversation with Beatrice
Galilee
September 29, 2015

Reading and Performance
*Topical Cream Magazine
Presents: Le Corbusier
Birthday Jam*, with Cecilia
Corrigan, Juliana Huxtable,
Eileen Myles, and Julika
Rudelius
October 6, 2015

Conversation
Trash Talk: Annabelle Selldorf
in conversation with Felix
Burrichter
October 20, 2015

Lecture and Screening
Jean-Louis Cohen on
Le Corbusier
November 3, 2015

Performance
Nina Beier: *Anti-Ageing*
November 7 and 8, 2015

IT'S PERFECT FOR LIVE STREAMING.
THIS ADJUSTABLE WET BAR IS THE PERFECT HAPPY HOUR COMPANION.
OH YES, THAT ANGLE LOOKS GOOD TOO.
BYE-BYE FOR NOW!
SO, IF YOU'RE INTERESTED IN BUYING ONE OF OUR FANTASTIC UNITS, YOU'D BETTER HURRY UP- THERE ARE ONLY FOUR LEFT, AND THEY COULD BE YOURS SOON. DON'T WASTE ANY TIME! MY EMAIL ADDRESS IS TRISH@ SWISSINSTITUTE.NET.

Contributors

FELIX BURRICHTER is a German-born, New York-based creative director and editor. He curated the second Architecture and Design exhibition, *PAVILLON DE L'ESPRIT NOUVEAU: A 21st Century Show Home,* at the Swiss Institute, New York (2015), and *Paper Weight: Genre-Defining Magazines 2000 to Now* at Haus der Kunst, Munich (2013). In 2017 the artist Andreas Angelidakis invited Burrichter to curate ten innovative design benches in a public park in Järfälla, Sweden. In 2017 for Rizzoli he coedited *Rafael de Cárdenas/Architecture at Large* with Karen Marta and wrote *Cassina: This Will Be the Place: Thoughts and Photographs about the Future of Interiors* in collaboration with Cassina, the Italian furniture-design company. He studied architecture at the Ecole Spéciale d'Architecture and Ecole Nationale Supérieure d'Architecture de Paris-Belleville in Paris and Columbia University in New York before founding *PIN-UP* magazine in 2006, where he is editor and creative director.

CARSON CHAN is an architecture writer and curator. In 2006 he founded PROGRAM, a Berlin-based residency and project space. He cocurated *Reaper: Sigfried Giedion, Richard Hamilton,* a collaborative exhibition cohosted by gta Exhibitions and the Graphische Sammlung, Zurich (2017); guest-curated at Aurora Dallas (2015); was executive curator of the Biennial of the Americas, Denver (2013); and curated the 4th Marrakech Biennale (2012). Chan has also written widely on art and architecture, with monographic texts on Barkow Leibinger, Paolo Chiasera, Monica Bonvicini, and Eva Grubinger. Chan is a PhD candidate at Princeton School of Architecture. His dissertation considers postwar American aquariums as models of ecology.

TRISH GOFF is a model turned real-estate agent. Her modeling led her to work with photographers such as Richard Avedon, Arthur Elgort, Peter Lindbergh, Steven Meisel, and Juergen Teller, and she was featured on the covers of *Vogue*, *Elle*, and *Cosmopolitan*. As a real-estate agent in New York she currently works for Compass, where she cofounded the Urbane Properties Team. A collector of contemporary art, Goff is also a cofounder of #knotonmyplanet, a campaign to provide a secure future for elephants by raising funds for the Elephant Crisis Fund.

MARC MATCHAK is a writer and painter based in Ridgewood, Queens. He received a Bachelor of Arts in English from Lewis & Clark College in Portland, Oregon. He has written for *PIN-UP* magazine and works as an editorial assistant for KMEC.

SHAWN MAXIMO is a New York-based artist and architect working in sculpture, digital media, and design. He has participated in exhibitions such as *Hello Robot* at the Vitra Design Museum in Weil am Rhein, Germany (2017); *Work it! Feel it!* at Kunsthalle Wien, Vienna (2017); *Open Codes* at ZKM Center for Art and Media in Karlsruhe, Germany (2017); *CO-WORKERS: Le réseau comme artiste* at Musée d'Art Moderne de la Ville de Paris (2015); and the 9th Berlin Biennale (2016). He received a dual master's degree in architecture and engineering from Princeton University.

Acknowledgments

PAVILLON DE L'ESPRIT NOUVEAU: A 21st Century Show Home is the marvelous result of Felix Burrichter's all-around brilliance. I am deeply grateful to him for his curatorial ingenuity, prescient insights, and unbridled enthusiasm throughout the development of the exhibition and in the process of creating this accompanying publication. His contributions have ensured that this book embodies *PDLEN's* wit, beauty, and innovation. His commitment to pushing boundaries took SI's Architecture and Design Series to a place I never thought possible. I must also thank Shawn Maximo, whose innovative exhibition design, technical precision, and artwork brought *PDLEN* to life.

To all the artists and designers who presented newly commissioned pieces or lent existing items, I am deeply grateful. It was an honor to be able to exhibit such outstanding examples of contemporary art and design. I must also thank the following lenders for their generosity: Aznom, Monza, Italy; Carpenter's Workshop Gallery, London and Paris; Cassina, Milan; Croy Nielsen, Berlin; Designtex, New York; Dzek Limited, London; Emeco, Hanover, Pennsylvania; Established & Sons, London; Expand Design LTD, London; Febrik, Tilburg, Netherlands; Flos, New York; Galerie Armel Soyer, Paris; Living Divani, Como, Italy; Nilufar Gallery, Milan; USM, New York; Vitra, Birsfelden, Switzerland; Volume Gallery, Chicago.

I would also like to thank all those who participated in the Le Corbusier Birthday Jam: Lyndsy Welgos and Topical Cream, Cecilia Corrigan, Juliana Huxtable, Eileen Myles, and Julika Rudelius. I am also deeply grateful to Beatrice Galilee, Annabelle Selldorf, Jean-Louis Cohen, and Nina Beier for their contributions to the exhibition's public programs and performances.

We were delighted to work with Pantone Color Institute, especially its vice president, Laurie Pressman, during the production of Sean Raspet's special edition for the exhibition. Her color matching and accompanying text for *Technical Food* and *Technical Milk* deeply enhanced Sean's project. Thanks to Riccardo Giraudi for his kind advocacy of Swiss Institute's idiosyncratic ideas.

I would also like to thank the exhibition's immensely generous supporters: Graham Foundation, Présence Suisse, Austrian Cultural Forum, Kara Mann, Danish Arts Foundation, and, last but certainly not least, Fondation Le Corbusier.

For their contributions to this book, I would like to thank Marc Matchak, Carson Chan, and our unstoppable sales agent, Trish Goff. Their enthusiastic participation in this publication was key to its success.

I must also thank the fantastic team at Karma, New York, for their generosity and commitment to excellence, especially Brendan Dugan, Sinisa Mackovic, and David Schoerner. I remain consistently inspired by their vision.

I am as grateful as ever to Karen Marta and her fantastic team of Todd Bradway and Tommaso Speretta for their editorial and production expertise. This book would not exist without their tireless efforts.

Lastly, I would like to thank our board of trustees and team at Swiss Institute, both past and present, particularly Alison Coplan, Laura McLean-Ferris, Clément Delépine, Scott Kiernan, Kristen Wawruck, Elizabeth Baribeau, Alexandra Zigrang, and Daniel Merritt, for their dedication to *PDLEN* and to our mission, and for their continued thoughtfulness.

   Simon Castets

Swiss Institute

Founded in 1986, Swiss Institute is an independent, nonprofit contemporary-art institution dedicated to promoting forward-thinking and experimental art-making through innovative exhibitions and programs. Committed to the highest standards of curatorial and educational excellence, Swiss Institute serves as a platform for emerging artists, catalyzes new contexts for celebrated work, and fosters appreciation for under-recognized positions.

Swiss Institute programming is made possible in part with public funds from Pro Helvetia; Swiss Arts Council; the New York State Council on the Arts, with the support of Governor Andrew Cuomo and the New York State Legislature; and the New York City Department of Cultural Affairs, in partnership with the City Council. Main sponsors include LUMA Foundation, the Andy Warhol Foundation for the Visual Arts, and Friends of Swiss Institute.

Swiss Institute gratefully acknowledges its Benefactors UBS and Stella Artois, Swiss Re as Public Programs Presenting Sponsor, Vitra as Design Partner, and SWISS as Travel Partner.

The SI Series

Embracing the conceptual framework of an exhibition at Swiss Institute and its related public programs, each book in the SI Series adds retrospective context through seminal essays, archival materials, event transcripts, artist portfolios, and exhibition documentation, as well as reprints and new translations of important texts.

OTHER TITLES IN THE SI SERIES

Allyson Vieira: The Plural Present
Heidi Bucher
The St. Petersburg Paradox
David Weiss: Works, 1968-1979
Work Hard: Selections by Valentin Carron
Niele Toroni
Fin de Siècle
Hans Schärer: Madonnas and Erotic Watercolors
FADE IN: INT. ART GALLERY - DAY
Sam Lewitt: Less Light Warm Words

Published for the exhibition
*PAVILLON DE L'ESPRIT NOUVEAU:
A 21st Century Show Home* at
Swiss Institute, New York,
September 25-November 8, 2015

© 2018 Swiss Institute, New
York; Karma, New York

Editors: Felix Burrichter,
Simon Castets, Karen Marta
Associate Editor: Alison Coplan
Managing Editor:
Tommaso Speretta
Editorial Assistant:
Marc Matchak
Copy Editor: Lawrence Levi
Production Advisor:
Todd Bradway
Initial design concept by
Studio Marie Lusa

Swiss Institute staff for
*PAVILLON DE L'ESPRIT NOUVEAU:
A 21st Century Show Home*:
Simon Castets, Elizabeth
Baribeau, Alexandra Zigrang,
Laura McLean-Ferris, Alison
Coplan, Daniel Merritt, Scott
Kiernan, Lisa Hamilton, Alex
LoRe
Volunteers: Andrew Alexander,
Ariela Braunschweig, James
Keller, Samantha Michel,
Marius Neuenschwander, Samira
Tanner
Installers: John McLaughlin,
Donals D'Aries, Victor De
Matha, Giles Hefferan

Lenders to the exhibition:
Aznom, Monza; Carpenter's
Workshop Gallery, London and
Paris; Cassina, Milan; Croy
Nielsen, Berlin; Designtex,
New York; Dzek Limited,
London; Emeco, Hanover;
Established & Sons, London;
Expand Design LTD, London;
Febrik, Tilburg; Flos, New
York; Galerie Armel Soyer,
Paris; Living Divani, Como;
Nilufar Gallery, Milan; USM,
New York; Vitra, Birsfelden;
Volume Gallery, Chicago

This book was made possible in
part by generous support from
Presence Suisse.

First published by:
Swiss Institute, New York;
Karma, New York

Swiss Institute
38 St Marks Pl
New York, NY 10003
Tel: + 1 212 925 2035
www.swissinstitute.net

Karma
188 East 2nd St.
New York, NY 10009
Tel: +1 917 675 7508
www.karmakarma.org

Every effort has been made to
contact copyright holders and
to obtain their permission for
the use of copyrighted material. Every effort has also
been made to provide accu-
rate information for all the
documented exhibitions. The

publishers apologize for any
errors or omissions and would
be grateful if notified of
any corrections that should
be incorporated in future
reprints or editions of this
publication.

Printed in Poland

ISBN: 978-0-9995059-1-5

Available through
ARTBOOK | D.A.P.
75 Broad St, Suite 630
New York, NY 10004
Tel.: +1(0) 212 627 1999
Fax: +1 (0) 212 627 9484
eleshowitz@dapinc.com

Cover image:
Katie Stout, *Lip Placemats*,
2015. Installation shot, Swiss
Institute, New York

TRISH GOFF

Exclusive agent for
PAVILLON DE L'ESPRIT NOUVEAU:
A 21st Century Show Home

SI

(212) 925-2035
trish@swissinstitute.net

"Everything I touch turns to SOLD!"

The End.

xxx

...looking for a new home.